THIS JOURNAL
BELONGS TO:

Visit us at www.journalforkids.com
or connect with us on Facebook at
Facebook.com/kidsjournals

~

We love hearing from you!

First Printing: 2019

ISBN 9781697628616

Journal for Kids
Freeport, Maine
www.journalforkids.com

Dear Parents and Caregivers,

If you are reading this, chances are you have a child that worries. As the parent of an anxious child you know how helpless you can feel, and so does your child. I've been there too, and I want to help you feel *hopeful* instead of *helpless*.

I created this journal along with my eight-year-old daughter, Ahna, who has struggled with anxiety her entire life.

With the help of many books, therapists, friends, and teachers, Ahna has successfully learned how to cope with her worries and shut down the worry bullies who take over every so often. It's been (and continues to be) a long, winding road and we are constantly teaching each other.

While anxiety will always be there, strategies such as breathing exercises and journaling have helped Ahna overcome her challenges and learn to effectively shut down the "worry monsters."

My hope for you is that using this journal will help open communication and create a safe space for you both to work through the challenges of anxiety.

I encourage you to be open to your child's feelings, listen, and understand that worries are not always logical, can come and go at the most unexpected times, and can be overcome with a lot of patience and time.

Ahna outlines worry and how to use this journal for your child on the following pages. I hope her experience will help your child understand that they are not alone and that they can push past the "worry monsters." Who better to hear it from than a peer!

Please note, this is not intended to replace any medical advice. We highly suggest contacting a trained professional if you feel your child would benefit from additional resources.

Once you find yourself needing the worry journal less, I encourage you to start a daily gratitude practice to continue improving your child's mindset. Thankful Thoughts is a self-exploration gratitude journal for kids that will help inspire your child to appreciate the little things, connect with their feelings and reflect on each day. **You can find this and all of our journals at** www.journalforkids.com.

Best of luck on your journey,
Stacey

How to use this Journal

by Ahna, age 8

Are you a kid that worries? Do you want to get rid of worries?

When you get that nervous, scary feeling you may feel a little bit sick sometimes. You may have a headache, your heart may start beating fast or your tummy may feel funny. That is worry trying to be a bully to you. It's trying to make you feel uncomfortable and scared. Worry does not want you to be happy.

Worry comes when you're thinking too hard and you start to think about scary things that might happen or go wrong. Some of the things I worry about are bees, dogs, fire, talking to new people and new experiences. You may be able to relate!

You might think this is crazy, but the worry is sometimes helpful because if you didn't have a worry you could get injured or make a big mistake. For example, if you jumped off the deck you could break your arm. Worry tells you to stop what you're doing and think this through. Will this hurt me? Is this not right?

Sometimes worry is not helpful because you can miss out on a lot of opportunities. There could be a sleepover at your friend's house, but you're so nervous you don't want to go. You may have the opportunity to try out for your school play, but you're so scared you miss out!

Your Brain

Do you want to understand why you worry? Your brain works in many different ways and there are a lot of different parts of it. I'm going to tell you a few parts of your brain that effect worries.

The first part of your brain is the prefrontal cortex. It's a long word. The prefrontal cortex is the part of your brain that makes decisions and it's sort of in charge of your brain.The second part of your brain is the amygdala. This is the part of your brain that is sort of like the bad guy. That is where worry lives. That's the part of your brain that is trying to keep the prefrontal cortex from using logic and reason.

Our job is to keep the amygdala from taking control. We want to keep both the prefrontal cortex and the amygdala in balance so they can both do their jobs. I'm going to give you some tips on how to to do that.

How to get rid of worry

To get rid of worry there are a few steps that have helped me.

- Take a deep breath. Take ten if you need to! Taking breaths can calm your body down.
- Stop what you're doing and start to think it through. Is this a big problem or a small problem? Then you have to say to yourself that you can do this!
- Say to worry "get lost" in your head. Say it over and over again!
- Find a safe place where you feel comfortable.
- Write your worries down.

These 5 steps can really help you get rid of worry. If you do it every time worries try to bully you, you could start to make worry pack up all his things and leave your brain!

Who to talk to

When you are worried you need someone to talk to. The people you should talk to are your Mom, Dad, Grandparents, or Teachers. They're like superheroes because they help make worries stop. They help you talk it through and remind you to take a deep breath.

Mom and Dad worry too. All grown-ups worry! Everybody worries! So don't feel like you're the only person in the world who worries, because you're not.

Parents aren't the only people who can help you. There are also "feelings teachers." They are special teachers who can help you stop worrying. They help you understand where your feelings are coming from and how to use coping skills so you can feel more comfortable.

I know I said your parents can help you but they're just helping, you're the one doing all the work. Because you should be the one doing all the work! Your parents can't just make worries go away in a flash. It takes time and hard work.

How to use this journal

The last step I mentioned was writing worries down. It's easy to let worry control us and worry all day long, but we aren't going to let that happen. We are going to set aside 20 minutes each day to use our journals and talk to our parents about worry. If you're feeling worried during the day, remind yourself that there will be time later to write it down and work through it with your parents if you want to.

Hey parents! Sometimes we just don't feel like talking about it, so don't push us! We can write in our worry journal all by ourselves too!

Today I'm Feeling:

Each page has these cool emojis on them! Use them to think about how you're feeling that day and circle the one that best matches your feelings. Sometimes we are having lots of feelings, so it's okay to pick more than one!

My worries:

Next, you can write down your worries or draw a picture of them. Or you can do both! Getting your worries out on paper will help you.

Talking back to my worries:

Once you've put your worries on paper I want you to tell your amygdala to stop trying to bully you and write down what you're going to say to that worry so it can't control you.

I'm proud of myself for talking back to these worries:

Lastly, it's important to be proud of yourself for using this journal and working hard to fight against your worries. Write down any worries that are in the past. If you don't have anything to write down here yet, don't worry. You will!

Getting my worries out on paper really helps me! I hope it helps you too! Don't forget, worry has a habit of sneaking up on you (sometimes when you least expect it) so keep writing down your worries and practicing talking back to them.

If your worries start to sneak back in, don't worry. That happens to me sometimes too. That's when I have to remind myself to use the strategies I've learned, take some deep breaths and talk back to my worries again and again!

You can do this!

Today's Date: _____

Today I'm feeling: 😄 😬 😠 😍 🙁 😳

My worries:

_____

_____

_____

_____

A picture of my worries:

Talking back to my worries:

My worries can't control me!

I'm proud of myself for talking back to these worries:

_____

Today's Date: _____

Today I'm feeling: 😄 😬 😠 😍 😟 😳

My worries:

_____

_____

_____

_____

A picture of my worries:

Talking back to my worries:

My worries can't control me!

I'm proud of myself for talking back to these worries:

_____

Today's Date: _____

Today I'm feeling:

My worries:

_____

_____

_____

_____

A picture of my worries:

Talking back to my worries:

My worries can't control me!

I'm proud of myself for talking back to these worries:

_____

Today's Date: _____

Today I'm feeling: 😄 😬 😠 😍 🙁 🥹

My worries:

_____

_____

_____

_____

A picture of my worries:

Talking back to my worries:

My worries can't control me!

I'm proud of myself for talking back to these worries:

_____

Today's Date: _____

Today I'm feeling: 😄 😬 😠 😍 🙁 😰

My worries:

_____

_____

_____

_____

A picture of my worries:

Talking back to my worries:

My worries can't control me!

I'm proud of myself for talking back to these worries:

_____

Today's Date: _____

Today I'm feeling:

My worries:

_____

_____

_____

_____

A picture of my worries:

Talking back to my worries:

My worries can't control me!

I'm proud of myself for talking back to these worries:

_____

Today's Date: _____

Today I'm feeling:

My worries:

_____

_____

_____

_____

A picture of my worries:

Talking back to my worries:

My worries can't control me!

I'm proud of myself for talking back to these worries:

_____

Today's Date: _____

Today I'm feeling:

My worries:

_____
_____
_____
_____

A picture of my worries:

Talking back to my worries:

My worries can't control me!

I'm proud of myself for talking back to these worries:

_____

Today's Date: _____

Today I'm feeling:

My worries:

_____

_____

_____

_____

A picture of my worries:

Talking back to my worries:

My worries can't control me!

I'm proud of myself for talking back to these worries:

_____

Today's Date: _____

Today I'm feeling:

My worries:

_____

_____

_____

_____

A picture of my worries:

Talking back to my worries:

My worries can't control me!

I'm proud of myself for talking back to these worries:

_____

Today's Date: _____

Today I'm feeling: 😅 😬 😠 😍 🙁 🫠

My worries:

_____

_____

_____

_____

A picture of my worries:

Talking back to my worries:

My worries can't control me!

I'm proud of myself for talking back to these worries:

_____

Today's Date: _____

Today I'm feeling: 😄 😬 😠 😍 🙁 🥺

My worries:

_____

_____

_____

_____

A picture of my worries:

Talking back to my worries:

My worries can't control me!

I'm proud of myself for talking back to these worries:

_____

Today's Date: _____

Today I'm feeling: 😄 😬 😠 😍 😔 😵

My worries:

_____

_____

_____

_____

A picture of my worries:

Talking back to my worries:

My worries can't control me!

I'm proud of myself for talking back to these worries:

_____

Today's Date: _____

Today I'm feeling: 😄 😬 😠 😍 🙁 😳

My worries:

_____

_____

_____

_____

A picture of my worries:

Talking back to my worries:

My worries can't control me!

I'm proud of myself for talking back to these worries:

_____

Today's Date: _____

Today I'm feeling:

My worries:

_____

_____

_____

_____

A picture of my worries:

Talking back to my worries:

My worries can't control me!

I'm proud of myself for talking back to these worries:

_____

Today's Date: _____

Today I'm feeling:

My worries:

_____

_____

_____

_____

A picture of my worries:

Talking back to my worries:

My worries can't control me!

I'm proud of myself for talking back to these worries:

_____

Today's Date: _____

Today I'm feeling: 😄 😬 😠 😍 😐 😳

My worries:

_____
_____
_____
_____

A picture of my worries:

Talking back to my worries:

My worries can't control me!

I'm proud of myself for talking back to these worries:

_____

Today's Date: _____

Today I'm feeling:

My worries:

_____

_____

_____

_____

A picture of my worries:

Talking back to my worries:

My worries can't control me!

I'm proud of myself for talking back to these worries:

_____

Today's Date: _____

Today I'm feeling:

My worries:

_____

_____

_____

_____

A picture of my worries:

Talking back to my worries:

My worries can't control me!

I'm proud of myself for talking back to these worries:

_____

Today's Date: _____

Today I'm feeling:

My worries:

_____

_____

_____

_____

A picture of my worries:

Talking back to my worries:

My worries can't control me!

I'm proud of myself for talking back to these worries:

_____

Today's Date: _____

Today I'm feeling: 😄 😬 😠 😍 😢 🥺

My worries:

_____

_____

_____

_____

A picture of my worries:

Talking back to my worries:

My worries can't control me!

I'm proud of myself for talking back to these worries:

_____

Today's Date: _____

Today I'm feeling: 😄 😬 😠 😍 😔 😳

My worries:

_____

_____

_____

_____

A picture of my worries:

Talking back to my worries:

My worries can't control me!

I'm proud of myself for talking back to these worries:

_____

Today's Date: _____

Today I'm feeling:

My worries:

_____

_____

_____

_____

A picture of my worries:

Talking back to my worries:

My worries can't control me!

I'm proud of myself for talking back to these worries:

_____

Today's Date: _____

Today I'm feeling: 😄 😬 😠 😍 😐 😳

My worries:

_____

_____

_____

_____

A picture of my worries:

Talking back to my worries:

My worries can't control me!

I'm proud of myself for talking back to these worries:

_____

Today's Date: _____

Today I'm feeling:

My worries:

_____

_____

_____

_____

A picture of my worries:

Talking back to my worries:

My worries can't control me!

I'm proud of myself for talking back to these worries:

_____

Today's Date: _____

Today I'm feeling: 😄 😬 😠 😍 😐 😳

My worries:

_____

_____

_____

_____

A picture of my worries:

Talking back to my worries:

My worries can't control me!

I'm proud of myself for talking back to these worries:

_____

Today's Date: _____

Today I'm feeling: 😄 😬 😠 😍 😢 🥶

My worries:

_____

_____

_____

_____

A picture of my worries:

Talking back to my worries:

My worries can't control me!

I'm proud of myself for talking back to these worries:

_____

Today's Date: _____

Today I'm feeling: 😄 😬 😠 😍 🙁 🥺

My worries:

_____

_____

_____

_____

A picture of my worries:

Talking back to my worries:

My worries can't control me!

I'm proud of myself for talking back to these worries:

_____

Today's Date: _____

Today I'm feeling: 😄 😬 😠 😍 😕 🥴

My worries:

_____

_____

_____

_____

A picture of my worries:

Talking back to my worries:

My worries can't control me!

I'm proud of myself for talking back to these worries:

_____

Today's Date: _____

Today I'm feeling:

My worries:

_____

_____

_____

_____

A picture of my worries:

Talking back to my worries:

My worries can't control me!

I'm proud of myself for talking back to these worries:

_____

Today's Date: _____

Today I'm feeling: 😄 😬 😠 😍 😐 😳

My worries:

_____

_____

_____

_____

A picture of my worries:

Talking back to my worries:

My worries can't control me!

I'm proud of myself for talking back to these worries:

_____

Today's Date: _____

Today I'm feeling:

My worries:

_____

_____

_____

_____

A picture of my worries:

Talking back to my worries:

My worries can't control me!

I'm proud of myself for talking back to these worries:

_____

Today's Date: _____

Today I'm feeling: 😄 😬 😠 😍 😐 😳

My worries:

_____

_____

_____

_____

A picture of my worries:

Talking back to my worries:

My worries can't control me!

I'm proud of myself for talking back to these worries:

_____

Today's Date: _____

Today I'm feeling: 😋 😬 😠 😍 😐 😳

My worries:

_____

_____

_____

_____

A picture of my worries:

Talking back to my worries:

My worries can't control me!

I'm proud of myself for talking back to these worries:

_____

Today's Date: _____

Today I'm feeling: 😄 😬 😠 😍 😐 😳

My worries:

_____

_____

_____

_____

A picture of my worries:

Talking back to my worries:

My worries can't control me!

I'm proud of myself for talking back to these worries:

_____

Today's Date: _____

Today I'm feeling:

My worries:

_____

_____

_____

_____

A picture of my worries:

Talking back to my worries:

My worries can't control me!

I'm proud of myself for talking back to these worries:

_____

Today's Date: _____

Today I'm feeling: 😄 😬 😠 😍 🙁 🥵

My worries:

_____

_____

_____

_____

A picture of my worries:

Talking back to my worries:

My worries can't control me!

I'm proud of myself for talking back to these worries:

_____

Today's Date: _____

Today I'm feeling:

My worries:

_____

_____

_____

_____

A picture of my worries:

Talking back to my worries:

My worries can't control me!

I'm proud of myself for talking back to these worries:

_____

Today's Date: _____

Today I'm feeling: 😄 😬 😠 😍 🙁 😰

My worries:

_____

_____

_____

_____

A picture of my worries:

Talking back to my worries:

My worries can't control me!

I'm proud of myself for talking back to these worries:

_____

Today's Date: _____

Today I'm feeling:

My worries:

_____

_____

_____

_____

A picture of my worries:

Talking back to my worries:

My worries can't control me!

I'm proud of myself for talking back to these worries:

_____

Today's Date: _____

Today I'm feeling: 😄 😬 😠 😍 😔 🥹

My worries:

_____

_____

_____

_____

A picture of my worries:

Talking back to my worries:

My worries can't control me!

I'm proud of myself for talking back to these worries:

_____

Today's Date: _____

Today I'm feeling:

My worries:

_____

_____

_____

_____

A picture of my worries:

Talking back to my worries:

My worries can't control me!

I'm proud of myself for talking back to these worries:

_____

Today's Date: _____

Today I'm feeling: 😄 😬 😠 😍 😕 🥵

My worries:

_____

_____

_____

_____

A picture of my worries:

Talking back to my worries:

My worries can't control me!

I'm proud of myself for talking back to these worries:

_____

Today's Date: _____

Today I'm feeling: 😄 😬 😠 😍 🙁 😳

My worries:

_____

_____

_____

_____

A picture of my worries:

Talking back to my worries:

My worries can't control me!

I'm proud of myself for talking back to these worries:

_____

Today's Date: _____

Today I'm feeling: 😄 😬 😠 😍 🙁 😰

My worries:

_____

_____

_____

_____

A picture of my worries:

Talking back to my worries:

My worries can't control me!

I'm proud of myself for talking back to these worries:

_____

Today's Date: _____

Today I'm feeling: 😄 😬 😠 😍 🙁 😨

My worries:

_____

_____

_____

_____

A picture of my worries:

Talking back to my worries:

My worries can't control me!

I'm proud of myself for talking back to these worries:

_____

Today's Date: _____

Today I'm feeling: 😄 😬 😠 😍 🙁 😰

My worries:

_____

_____

_____

_____

A picture of my worries:

Talking back to my worries:

My worries can't control me!

I'm proud of myself for talking back to these worries:

_____

Today's Date: _____

Today I'm feeling: 😄 😬 😠 😍 🙁 😳

My worries:

_____

_____

_____

_____

A picture of my worries:

Talking back to my worries:

My worries can't control me!

I'm proud of myself for talking back to these worries:

_____

Today's Date: _____

Today I'm feeling:

My worries:

_____

_____

_____

_____

A picture of my worries:

Talking back to my worries:

My worries can't control me!

I'm proud of myself for talking back to these worries:

_____

Today's Date: _____

Today I'm feeling: 😄 😬 😠 😍 😔 😳

My worries:

_____

_____

_____

_____

A picture of my worries:

Talking back to my worries:

My worries can't control me!

I'm proud of myself for talking back to these worries:

_____

Today's Date: _____

Today I'm feeling: 😊 😬 😠 😍 🙁 😱

My worries:

_____

_____

_____

_____

A picture of my worries:

Talking back to my worries:

My worries can't control me!

I'm proud of myself for talking back to these worries:

_____

Today's Date: _____

Today I'm feeling: 😄 😬 😠 😍 😟 😳

My worries:

_____

_____

_____

_____

A picture of my worries:

Talking back to my worries:

My worries can't control me!

I'm proud of myself for talking back to these worries:

_____

Today's Date: _____

Today I'm feeling: 😄 😬 😠 😍 😕 🥶

My worries:

_____

_____

_____

_____

A picture of my worries:

Talking back to my worries:

My worries can't control me!

I'm proud of myself for talking back to these worries:

_____

Today's Date: _____

Today I'm feeling:

My worries:

_____

_____

_____

_____

A picture of my worries:

Talking back to my worries:

My worries can't control me!

I'm proud of myself for talking back to these worries:

_____

Today's Date: _____

Today I'm feeling: 😊 😬 😠 😍 😕 🤐

My worries:

_____

_____

_____

_____

A picture of my worries:

Talking back to my worries:

My worries can't control me!

I'm proud of myself for talking back to these worries:

_____

Today's Date: _____

Today I'm feeling: 😄 😬 😠 😍 😕 😳

My worries:

_____

_____

_____

_____

A picture of my worries:

Talking back to my worries:

My worries can't control me!

I'm proud of myself for talking back to these worries:

_____

Today's Date: _____

Today I'm feeling: 😄 😬 😠 😍 🙁 🥹

My worries:

_____

_____

_____

_____

A picture of my worries:

Talking back to my worries:

My worries can't control me!

I'm proud of myself for talking back to these worries:

_____

Today's Date: _____

Today I'm feeling: 😄 😬 😠 😍 🙁 😳

My worries:

_____

_____

_____

_____

A picture of my worries:

Talking back to my worries:

My worries can't control me!

I'm proud of myself for talking back to these worries:

_____

Today's Date: _____

Today I'm feeling:

My worries:

_____

_____

_____

_____

A picture of my worries:

Talking back to my worries:

My worries can't control me!

I'm proud of myself for talking back to these worries:

_____

Today's Date: _____

Today I'm feeling: 😄 😬 😠 😍 😕 😳

My worries:

_____

_____

_____

_____

A picture of my worries:

Talking back to my worries:

My worries can't control me!

I'm proud of myself for talking back to these worries:

_____

Today's Date: _____

Today I'm feeling: 😄 😬 😠 😍 😔 🤪

My worries:

_____

_____

_____

_____

A picture of my worries:

Talking back to my worries:

My worries can't control me!

I'm proud of myself for talking back to these worries:

_____

Today's Date: _____

Today I'm feeling:

My worries:

_____

_____

_____

_____

A picture of my worries:

Talking back to my worries:

My worries can't control me!

I'm proud of myself for talking back to these worries:

_____

Today's Date: _____

Today I'm feeling: 😄 😬 😠 😍 🙁 😳

My worries:

_____

_____

_____

_____

A picture of my worries:

Talking back to my worries:

My worries can't control me!

I'm proud of myself for talking back to these worries:

_____

Today's Date: _____

Today I'm feeling: 😄 😬 😠 😍 🙁 😳

My worries:

_____

_____

_____

_____

A picture of my worries:

Talking back to my worries:

My worries can't control me!

I'm proud of myself for talking back to these worries:

_____

Today's Date: _____

Today I'm feeling:

My worries:

_____

_____

_____

_____

A picture of my worries:

Talking back to my worries:

My worries can't control me!

I'm proud of myself for talking back to these worries:

_____

Today's Date: _____

Today I'm feeling: 😄 😬 😠 😍 😕 😳

My worries:

_____

_____

_____

_____

A picture of my worries:

Talking back to my worries:

My worries can't control me!

I'm proud of myself for talking back to these worries:

_____

Today's Date: _____

Today I'm feeling:

My worries:

_____

_____

_____

_____

A picture of my worries:

Talking back to my worries:

My worries can't control me!

I'm proud of myself for talking back to these worries:

_____

Today's Date: _____

Today I'm feeling: 😄 😬 😠 😍 🙁 😳

My worries:

_____

_____

_____

_____

A picture of my worries:

Talking back to my worries:

My worries can't control me!

I'm proud of myself for talking back to these worries:

_____

Today's Date: _____

Today I'm feeling: 😄 😬 😠 😍 🙁 😰

My worries:

_____

_____

_____

_____

A picture of my worries:

Talking back to my worries:

My worries can't control me!

I'm proud of myself for talking back to these worries:

_____

Today's Date: _____

Today I'm feeling: 😄 😬 😠 😍 🙁 😳

My worries:

_____

_____

_____

_____

A picture of my worries:

Talking back to my worries:

My worries can't control me!

I'm proud of myself for talking back to these worries:

_____

Today's Date: _____

Today I'm feeling:

My worries:

_____

_____

_____

_____

A picture of my worries:

Talking back to my worries:

My worries can't control me!

I'm proud of myself for talking back to these worries:

_____

Today's Date: _____

Today I'm feeling:

My worries:

_____

_____

_____

_____

A picture of my worries:

Talking back to my worries:

My worries
can't control
me!

I'm proud of myself for talking back to these worries:

_____

Today's Date: _____

Today I'm feeling: 😀 😬 😠 😍 😕 😳

My worries:

_____

_____

_____

_____

A picture of my worries:

Talking back to my worries:

My worries can't control me!

I'm proud of myself for talking back to these worries:

_____

Today's Date: _____

Today I'm feeling: 😄 😬 😠 😍 🙁 😳

My worries:

_____

_____

_____

_____

A picture of my worries:

Talking back to my worries:

My worries can't control me!

I'm proud of myself for talking back to these worries:

_____

Today's Date: _____

Today I'm feeling:

My worries:

_____

_____

_____

_____

A picture of my worries:

Talking back to my worries:

My worries can't control me!

I'm proud of myself for talking back to these worries:

_____

Today's Date: _____

Today I'm feeling:

My worries:

_____

_____

_____

_____

A picture of my worries:

Talking back to my worries:

My worries can't control me!

I'm proud of myself for talking back to these worries:

_____

Today's Date: _____

Today I'm feeling:

My worries:

_____

_____

_____

_____

A picture of my worries:

Talking back to my worries:

My worries can't control me!

I'm proud of myself for talking back to these worries:

_____

Today's Date: _____

Today I'm feeling:

My worries:

_____

_____

_____

_____

A picture of my worries:

Talking back to my worries:

My worries can't control me!

I'm proud of myself for talking back to these worries:

_____

Today's Date: _____

Today I'm feeling:

My worries:

_____

_____

_____

_____

A picture of my worries:

Talking back to my worries:

My worries can't control me!

I'm proud of myself for talking back to these worries:

_____

Today's Date: _____

Today I'm feeling:

My worries:

_____

_____

_____

_____

A picture of my worries:

Talking back to my worries:

My worries can't control me!

I'm proud of myself for talking back to these worries:

_____

Today's Date: _____

Today I'm feeling: 😄 😬 😠 😍 😕 😳

My worries:

_____

_____

_____

_____

A picture of my worries:

Talking back to my worries:

My worries can't control me!

I'm proud of myself for talking back to these worries:

_____

Today's Date: _____

Today I'm feeling: 😄 😬 😠 😍 🙁 😰

My worries:

_____

_____

_____

_____

A picture of my worries:

Talking back to my worries:

My worries can't control me!

I'm proud of myself for talking back to these worries:

_____

Today's Date: _____

Today I'm feeling: 😅 😬 😠 😍 😕 🥴

My worries:

_____

_____

_____

_____

A picture of my worries:

Talking back to my worries:

My worries can't control me!

I'm proud of myself for talking back to these worries:

_____

Today's Date: _____

Today I'm feeling: 😄 😬 😠 😍 😕 😳

My worries:

_____

_____

_____

_____

A picture of my worries:

Talking back to my worries:

My worries can't control me!

I'm proud of myself for talking back to these worries:

_____

Today's Date: _____

Today I'm feeling:

My worries:

_____

_____

_____

_____

A picture of my worries:

Talking back to my worries:

My worries can't control me!

I'm proud of myself for talking back to these worries:

_____

Today's Date: _____

Today I'm feeling: 😄 😬 😠 😍 🙁 😳

My worries:

_____

_____

_____

_____

A picture of my worries:

Talking back to my worries:

My worries can't control me!

I'm proud of myself for talking back to these worries:

_____

Today's Date: _____

Today I'm feeling: 😄 😬 😠 😍 🙁 😳

My worries:

_____

_____

_____

_____

A picture of my worries:

Talking back to my worries:

My worries can't control me!

I'm proud of myself for talking back to these worries:

_____

Today's Date: _____

Today I'm feeling: 😄 😬 😠 😍 😐 😳

My worries:

_____

_____

_____

_____

A picture of my worries:

Talking back to my worries:

My worries can't control me!

I'm proud of myself for talking back to these worries:

_____

Today's Date: _____

Today I'm feeling:

My worries:

_____

_____

_____

_____

A picture of my worries:

Talking back to my worries:

My worries can't control me!

I'm proud of myself for talking back to these worries:

_____

Today's Date: _____

Today I'm feeling: 😄 😬 😠 😍 😢 😳

My worries:

_____

_____

_____

_____

A picture of my worries:

Talking back to my worries:

My worries can't control me!

I'm proud of myself for talking back to these worries:

_____

Great job talking back to your worries! Don't forget to remind your parents to order your next journal at **www.journalforkids.com**

Made in the USA
Middletown, DE
06 September 2021

47693904R00056